Cradle of Love
A Tribute to Metropolitan Moms

English Language
Cradle of Love
A Tribute to Metropolitan Moms
(Anthology)
Compiled by
Metropolitan International Indian School, Ajman

Published in November 2024
by Decan Imprint Publishing Co.
Reg. Off: Sharjah Publishing City
Free Zone Sharjah, UAE.
Phone: 00971-561127998
Email : decanimprint@gmail.com

Cover Design : Hamdan. K, Grade: 7E

All the images in the book are captured by the author, unless otherwise
specified, and the author holds the copyright for such images.

AED 27
20/24-25/Sl.No.20/140/NS 15.4
ISBN 978-93-5973-824-6

Cradle of Love
A Tribute to Metropolitan Moms

Metropolitan International Indian School, Ajman

DECANIMPRINT

"To all the mothers who cradle the world with love…….."

Foreword

It is with great pride and heartfelt emotion that I present to you *'Cradle of Love: A Tribute to Metropolitan Moms'*, a beautiful anthology of poems written by the talented students of Metropolitan International Indian School. This collection is a tribute to one of the purest forms of love—the love of a mother.

As educators, we strive to nurture creativity and compassion in our students, encouraging them to explore the depths of their emotions through artistic expression. Cradle of Love is a testament to their ability to articulate the unique and powerful bond between mother and child. Through each poem, they have captured the essence of what it means to be loved, nurtured, and cared for unconditionally.

This book is not only a reflection of our students' creative potential but also a tribute to the mothers who have been their guiding lights. As they weave words into verses, they honor the sacrifices, strength, and undying affection that every mother so generously provides. It is a token of appreciation to all Metropolitan moms, whose love forms the foundation upon which the future is built.

I am deeply honoured that this first book launch is being

celebrated at the prestigious Sharjah International Book Fair. It is a significant milestone for our school and a moment of pride for our entire community.

May these poems remind us of the eternal bond between mother and child and serve as a beacon of love, compassion, and inspiration for all who read them.

With warmest regards,
Dr. Abdul Majeed
Principal
Metropolitan International Indian School, Ajman

Preface

With a heart full of gratitude and admiration, I present to you **'Cradle of Love: A Tribute to Metropolitan Moms',** a tender collection of poems that speaks to the timeless bond between a mother and her child. Each verse, carefully penned by the students of Metropolitan International Indian School, is a tribute to the quiet strength, the boundless affection, and the unquestionable devotion that only a mother can give.

This anthology would not have bloomed without the tireless dedication of our English department. Your dedication, your attention to the finest of details, and your passion for this work have left an indelible mark on this collection. You have helped shape these poems into more than just words on a page; they are living expressions of love and gratitude.

A special acknowledgment goes to our Chief Editor, Ms. Rahba. Like a careful gardener, she has nurtured this project from its inception, ensuring that each poem, each word, is a faithful reflection of a child's love for their mother. Her keen eye and steady hand have shaped this collection into something truly beautiful.

My sincere appreciation to our brilliant student editors, Emin Rose and Adhi Dev.

'Cradle of Love: A Tribute to Metropolitan Moms' is not merely a collection of poems—it is a song of the heart, a whispered thank you to every mother whose love forms the very essence of our being. May these poems touch you, as they have touched us, with their purity and warmth.

With all my heart,
Ms. Nancy K Anto
Vice Principal
Metropolitan International Indian School, Ajman

Chief Editor's Message

It is with sincere gratitude and great delight that I present to you this anthology, '*Cradle of Love: A Tribute to Metropolitan Moms*', a heartfelt collection of poems on the beautiful theme of Mother's Love, crafted by the talented students of Metropolitan International Indian School, Ajman. As part of our Mother's Day celebrations, we invited students to express their thoughts and emotions through poetry, and the response has been overwhelming. Each poem in this collection is a heartfelt tribute to the unique and unconditional love that mothers provide. The creativity and emotional depth shown by our young poets are truly inspiring.

I would like to extend my sincere gratitude to the dedicated teachers of the English Department, who served as the editorial board for this anthology. Their hard work, meticulous attention to detail, and thoughtful guidance in editing and organizing the poems have played a key role in bringing this project to life.

I would also like to express my deepest gratitude to our respected Principal, Dr. Abdul Majeed, our Vice Principal, Ms. Nancy Paul, Boys' Section Headmaster, Mr. Abdul Shukkur, Girls' Section Headmistress, Ms. Nesiya Rahim, Primary Section Headmistress, Ms. Limla Suresh and Kindergarten Headmistress,

Ms. SubuThankachy for their unwavering support and guidance. Their encouragement and leadership have provided the foundation for this project's success, and we are incredibly grateful for their vision.

I hope that this anthology will not only inspire and uplift its readers but also serve as a lasting reminder of the enduring power of maternal love. May the words of these young poets resonate with you and evoke a sense of gratitude and appreciation for the extraordinary women in your lives.

Thank you to everyone involved in making this anthology a reality.

With boundless love,
RAHBA. P. S
Chief Editor,
Metropolitan International Indian School, Ajman

Student Editor's Note

Welcome to this special anthology, **'*Cradle of Love: A Tribute to Metropolitan Moms*',** created by the talented students of Metropolitan International Indian School, that celebrates the deep and unconditional love of mothers. Through these heartfelt poems, our young writers have beautifully captured the essence of a mother's love—nurturing, comforting, and shaping us in countless ways.

As you turn these pages, you will find yourself touched by the sincerity and depth of the students' reflections. Each poem explores different aspects of a mother's love, from tender moments of care to the quiet strength and resilience that mothers embody. These poems remind us of the profound impact our mothers have on shaping our lives and nurturing our dreams.

We are immensely grateful to the students who poured their hearts into these poems and to the teachers and staff who helped bring this project to life. Special thanks to the editorial team for their hard work and dedication in making this anthology possible. We hope that **'*Cradle of Love: A Tribute to Metropolitan Moms*'** stirs your heart and inspires you to reflect on the love and sacrifices of the incredible women we call "*Mom*."

With Warm Regards,
Adhi Dev Babu & Emin Rose
Student Editors,
Metropolitan International Indian School, Ajman.

Metropolitan International Indian Private School

Metropolitan International Indian Private School (MIIS) is a distinguished educational institution dedicated to fostering academic excellence, holistic development, and cultural enrichment. Sponsored by Shaikh Abdullah Bin Majid Al Nuaimi and established with the support of a diverse group of 200+ individuals passionate about education, MIIS is grounded in the vision of nurturing a generation of well-rounded individuals who embody universal values.

With a curriculum aligned with the Central Board of Secondary Education (CBSE), MIIS combines traditional Indian values with global perspectives, equipping students with essential 21st-century skills like critical thinking, creativity, communication, and collaboration. The school respects and integrates UAE values and cultural insights throughout the academic year, as guided by the Ministry of Education, making MIIS a blend of international standards and local respect.

MIIS features state-of-the-art facilities, including well-equipped classrooms, science and computer labs, libraries, and extensive sports areas, such as football and basketball courts, a swimming pool, and play areas for younger students. For Students of Determination, MIIS provides dedicated resource rooms to support their unique learning needs. The school also offers a mixed-gender environment for early years and primary students, transitioning to gender- segregated classes from Grade 5 to Grade 12 to better meet students' developmental stages.

Faculty at MIIS are committed to providing personalized attention and guidance, encouraging students to explore their interests through diverse academic programs, extracurricular activities, and community service. The school's open and inclusive admission policy fosters an environment where every student has the opportunity to thrive, grow, and contribute meaningfully to an interconnected world. Through its dynamic and supportive learning environment, MIIS aims to develop confident, compassionate, and responsible global citizens.

Sl.No.	Title of the Poem	Name of the child	Gr.	Div.	Page No.
20	Mother:The Icon of Love	Vaishnav. R	8	C	44
21	A Mother's Love Unspoken	Emin Rose	8	N	45
22	Mother's Heart	Alfie Steena	7	R	46
23	My Feelings For My Mom	Muhammed Armaan	7	A	47
24	Life Of Mother	Ayhath Sana Sideek	7	R	49
25	A Mother's True Love	Abdullah Farhan	7	A	50
26	A Mother's Love	Isabella sunil Mathew	7	P	52
27	I Love My Mom	Niya Jyothish	7	P	53
28	Mom, I Love You To The Moon	Haya Mohammed	7	R	54
29	Thank You!	Jiwel	7	N	55
30	Marvelous Mothers!	Ayaan Saju	7	F	56
31	Mom's Love: Our Guiding Light	Hina Farooke	7	N	57
32	My guiding light	Parvathi Vinesh Menon	7	R	58
33	My Mother	Aysha.M	7	M	59
34	Mommy	Nadha Fathima	7	P	60
35	Mother	Rahila Syed	7	R	61
36	Father and Mother: My World of Joy	S.Shithika	7	M	62
37	Happy Mother's Day	Sara Mohammed	6	N	64
38	My Mother	Aditi Vipin	6	M	65
39	My Mother	Ameen Zayed	6	D	66
40	My Guiding Light	Amila kaheesha	6	R	67
41	Mother	Amna Ahmed	6	N	68
42	Mother's Love	Ayshath Nasha	6	Q	69
43	Love You Mother	Dhiya Fathima	6	M	70

Sl.No.	Title of the Poem	Name of the child	Gr.	Div.	Page No.
44	My Mother	Filza Fathima	6	R	71
45	♥M•O•M♥	Muhamed Hamdan	6	E	72
46	Happy Mother' Day ♥	Niba Nourin	6	N	73
47	Mother Melody	Adam Zayn Arshid	6	A	74
48	Mother's Love : A Sonnet of Gratitude	Muskan.V.N	6	N	75
49	My Loving Mother	Aysha Fahima	6	R	76
50	My Mother	Kanika M Shetty	6	N	77
51	My Mother	Chinmaya Joji	6	Q	78
52	My Mother	Jaiveer	6	D	79
53	My Mother	Saira Mariam Ullas	6	P	80
54	Mother-a heaven on earth	Zoya Adnan	6	N	81
55	A Mothers Love Our Sweetest Gift	Divaritika Sureshkumar	5	R	82
56	Mother	Aliya Ahmed	5	P	83
57	Mom	Chris Simon Sumesh	5	E	84
58	My Mom	Alihamdan	5	F	85
59	Mom!!!	Verdil Samuel	5	H	87
60	Dear Mother	Aarush	5	F	88
61	Happy Mother's Day	Dishan Chandra	5	E	89
62	My Mother is a Butterfly	Fathimath Nazha .P	5	R	90
63	My Mom	Fayha firos	5	R	91
64	"Beats of My Heart"	Gaurinandhana.P.S	5	P	92
65	My Lovely Mother	Haani Muhammed	5	J	93
66	My Mother	Haniya fathima	5	R	94
67	My Mom	Krithika Rajesh	5	Q	95
68	My Mother	Mahd Rafan	5	G	96

SlNo.	Title of the Poem	Name of the child	Gr.	Div.	Page No.
69	Mother	Jiwon Jose	5	D	97
70	My Golden Solace	Ishan. M	5	D	99
71	My Mom	Dakshan.T.K	5	B	100
72	My Mother	Raizan Muhammed	5	J	101
73	My Mom	Natasha Parakkunnath	5	S	102
74	My Guiding Star - My Mom	Hrithik V	5	B	103
75	My Mother	Yuzaira Fathima	5	M	104
76	My Angel	Aaliya Sahid	4	G	105
77	Lovely Mom	Amreen Hajrah	4	P	107
78	My Mom	Anvid Jayin	4	H	108
79	My Mother	Isha Mehrin	4	R	109
80	Thank you, MOM	Haleema Beevi	4	A	111
81	Mom	Ayana Iqbal	4	E	112
82	I Love You Mommy Song	Fathima Naifah	4	E	113
83	My Sweet Mom	Sreeyuktha. K.S	4	J	115
84	My Mother My Star	Nidhi Ragesh	4	H	116
85	For You Mom..	Jinaan Bint Jaseel	4	R	117
86	My Mother a Blessing	Amaya Choudhary	4	M	118
87	My Mother	Lakshmi Reghunandanan	4	G	119
88	My Mother My Guardian	Ashlin Maria Anish	4	J	120
89	My Lovely Mother	Saiha T Sunil	4	G	121
90	My Wonderful Mother	Shanza Mehrin	4	E	122
91	To My Mom	Yuvraj Singh Mathru	4	M	123
92	Heart of a Mother	Annbriya Angel	4	M	124
93	My Mother	Affan Farhan	3	B	125
94	Amma	Manish Sudhakar	3	B	126

SlNo.	Title of the Poem	Name of the child	Gr.	Div.	Page No.
95	Mother	Aysha Ahmed	3	G	127
96	Mother's Day Song	Khadijah Waafiyah	3	N	128
97	My Mother, My Angel	Samrah Mahek	3	A	129
98	My dearest Mom	Dakshitha Rajil	3	F	130
99	My Lovely Mother	Aarush K.R	3	F	131
100	My Mom	Hanan Najim	3	D	132
101	My Mother is the Best	Fathima Ayra	3	D	133
102	My Mother	Vashisht.C.S	3	E	134
103	My Mother	Muhammed Haziq	3	M	135
104	My Mom, The Best	Mohammed Aahil Ghulam	3	N	137
105	My Lovely Mom	Fatimah zahra	3	D	138
106	My Mother	Danvin Nikhil	3	E	139
107	My Beloved Mother	Zunaira Mehwish	3	B	140

Manha Iqbal
8 R

MOM!

You have always been there for me when I needed you;
you're more than a friend in this whole world there are
many mothers; I am lucky and glad to be your child to
have such a nice mother!
you carry in your womb for nine months and you went
through a lot of pain! I will not let go of that pain and I
promise that I will be a proud daughter for you!
In the gentle glow of morning light! Your love, dear mama
shines so bright; through every joy and every tear; you've
been my rock, always near me!
Your hands have held me, Warm & strong, guiding me
when paths seem long in your embrace, I find my peace, A
love that never seems to cease!
Your words of wisdom, soft and true, have shaped my
world; my point of view in laughter shared & sorrows
known in you; I have never been alone;
With every hug and tender kiss, you have filled my life
with boundless bliss!

Your sacrifices countless, vast, have built my future from
the past;
So here; I open my grateful heart; in verses where
emotions start!
Thank you for your endless grace; your loving arms, my
safest place!
Forevermore; my love will grow, with every day, I will let
you know that, you're my guide;
Always by my side; you're my best mom!

A.Bhawyasri
8 R

"A HEARTFELT TRIBUTE TO MOM"

I love you so much, Mom,
For all that you do,
You help me grow strong and true.
"Mother" is a word so dear,
Your love shines bright, always near.
You nourish me and guide my way,
You're my best friend every day.
You're amazing, that's for sure,
To me, you're special and pure.

Abhinand Rajith Kumar
8 A

MOTHER'S DAY

God created a wonderful mother
My mother is my best friend
I will love you forever.

A very, very special person you are,
And you mean the world to me.
Day or night,
Sky or earth,
Sea or river,
Big or small,
Happy or sad—
It's all about you, mother.

Aboobakker Tashif
8 A

A MOTHER'S SACRIFICE

A mother's love, a sacrifice,
Her every act, a precious price.
She works from dawn to late at night,
To make our world so warm and bright.

Her dreams she sets upon a shelf,
To give us more than she has herself.
With tired eyes and weary hands,
She nurtures us, she understands.

She gives us strength, her own she hides,
In silent tears and sleepless nights.
Her hopes and wishes often wait,
For us, she changes her own fate.

In every hug and whispered cheer,
Her sacrifices shine so clear.
A mother's love, so deep and true,
She gives her all for me and you.

Sayyid Muhammad Faheem
8 E

THE WOMAN
WHO TAUGHT ME TO DREAM

My mom is an angel to me,
Who came as a savior to me.
My mom is the one
Who teaches me.

I am Mommy's little prince,
She is an angel to me.

"Mommy, Mommy, what is it?"
"It is the space shuttle, my prince."
"Where is it going?"
"It is going to Space."

"Mommy, Mommy,
Who is in it?"
"An astronaut is inside it."

"Can I become an astronaut?"
"You can be an astronaut."

"Thanks, Mommy. Good night."
"Good night, my little prince."

Fathima Mehra
8 Q

THE LIGHT OF MATERNAL LOVE

Nine painful divisions of the year,
Of Herself, nor did she care, neither did she fear.
Pain that would make one scream,
Once she saw me, O how brightly she beamed.
The warmth of motherhood,
Where blossomed the seed of love
For her own kind and,
For her kind's kind.
Watched over the steps to independence,
O dear mother, how much more would you do for me?
Thy touch holds the comfort,
Thy words soothe me somewhat.
Thou may not be God,
But thou art one form of love.
Motherly love, motherly touch,
Overcome the feeling of any grudge.

Isha Fathima.P
8 P

A PURE SOUL

My love for my mother will remain until my last breath!
Her heart is as soft as a rose petal,
Her love and care for us are sweeter than anything in the
world.
She guides us to the righteous path;
She motivates us.
When it comes to me, my mother is way too sensitive.
When I'm with her, she never gives me a chance to shed a
tear!
When no one is there, a mother will always be there for us
like a shadow of lightning, even though we have hurt her
many times.
Life without a mother... is unthinkable.

Sameeha
8 R

"ODE TO A MOTHER'S LOVE"

If a shoe is made of leather,
Then my life is made by my mother.
The word "mother" is not just a word;
It is everything, truth assured.
In my dreams, she comes as a princess,
Made of light beams and success.
She is a housewife, yet she shines
In my life, with love that defines.
She is the only one who truly cares,
The only one who always dares
To sacrifice, to give, to be
A guiding light for all to see.
She is a kind soul, with reasons grand,
A superwoman, a helping hand.
Mother, you're my guardian angel, too;
I love you, Mom, in all you do.

 'Cradle of Love: A Tribute to Metropolitan Moms'

Mohammed Rashdan
8 B

MOM

Mothers are the quiet strength that heals,
With hands that soothe and love that feels.
Their whispered words, a calming shore,
A heart that gives forever more.

In darkest times, they light the way,
Their warmth like dawn, chasing night away.
A mother's love, so vast, so deep,
In her embrace, our souls find peace

Hemachandran

8 C

THE ORIGIN OF US

In Mother's garden, where hearts bloom wide
A day for moms, with joy inside.
Their hugs, like cozy, warm embrace,
Their love, a light in all the places.

With arms that hold us, safe and tight,
For the day and night.
Their smiles, like sunshine, warm and bright
Guiding through the darkest night.

In every word, a caring touch,
In every action, oh so much.
Their love, a gift, simple and true,
Shining bright in all they do.

So, let's thank them, with hearts so light,
For making everything all right.
In their love, we find our way,
Happy Mother's day every single day.

Muhsin.A
8 A

MOM'S LOVE IN EVERY LINE

Hey Mom, it's your special day,
As the morning light begins to shine,
You send me off to school once more,
To learn, to grow, and spend time with friends of mine.

Walking home along the path,
I meet my friends, who can sometimes be unkind,
But the kindest people I know by far,
Are mothers, who are the finest you'll ever find.

Adwaith
8 C

MY LOVELY MOM

I love my mother!
She is the role model to me,
She cares for the whole family,
She is the sunshine in my life,
Sometimes like the moon.
She gives me something hot,
She gives me something cold.
If I am sad,
She also feels sad.
When I am happy,
She is happy too.
She is my teacher, friend, and doctor,
She plays every role in my life.
When she scolds, I feel pain,
But I know it is for my better life.
When she scolds me, her heart breaks.
She is my lovely mother,
I am so lucky and proud of her.

My mom, you are an angel
In my life.
I love you, Mom!

Mohammed Ridwan
8 C

MY MOM

My mother shines as my guiding light,
She is like a candle melting along my path.
Her grip is firm, for me a lifeline, never letting me drown,
She picked the stones and thorns in my way for forging
ahead.

In her eyes, I see a world of grace,
A mother's love, a sacred embrace.
Through every trial, she stands by my side,
In her love, I find my strength, my guide.

Her wisdom flows like a gentle stream,
Guiding me through life's complex scheme.
In her laughter, I find endless joy
Her kisses always make me happy.

In her embrace, I find comfort and strength,
When I'm wrapped in her arms, I feel safe.
With tender care, she soothes my fears,
She wipes my tears with her warm kisses.

Janish Mohammed
8 B

MY MOTHER

I love my mother
In the morning,
She is my sun.
I love my mother.
In tough situations,
She is my lifeline
I love my mother
Behind all my achievements,
There is my mother.
I love my mother.
In my life,
She is my all-rounder
I love my mother.

Muhammed Ajfan
8 A

MY MOM, MY HERO

My mom is kind, her hugs so warm,
In her embrace, I feel no harm.
She listens when I have to say,
She helps me through each tough day.

Her smile is like the shining sun,
Her love, a river, never done.
She cooks, she cleans, she's always there,
To show me that she truly cares.

On this day, I want to say,
Thank you, Mom, in every way.
You're my hero, you're my light,
In your arms, everything's all right.

Happy Mother's Day, I love you so,
You make my world a happy glow.

Filza Mehanaz
8 M

THE LIGHT AMONG SHADOWS: MOM

In the tapestry of love, she holds a special place.
Our hearts hold the mighty power,
To honor the ones who nurture and empower.
Her endless care, beyond compare.
The heart that's always there.
Each word a caress,
From the one who brings comfort in distress,
The one guiding us through life's shifting sands.
Ummi, I call in moments of joy and woe,
Through laughter and tears, she stands by my side,
sets my soul aglow.
For in her, a love forever bound,
Through trials and sacrifices made lifelong,
She stands, unwavering, strong.
Can't we spare some words as a beacon of
appreciation,
For the silent heroes of every generation?

Rimsha Basheer
8 P

MY MOTHER,
A CULINARY QUEEN!

My mother, oh so dear and fine,
A talent so rare, a heart so pure.
In every skill, she's a master too,
Her skills so fine, her smile so bright,
They leave me in awe.
Oh, my mother, a culinary queen,
Who makes the dish of the day.
She needs no comparison,
Her dishes are simply the best.
Her hands move splendidly,
Turning simple ingredients into
A culinary masterpiece.
Oh, what an artist she is, isn't she?
My mother, oh so talented and kind,
Her gifts so fine, her smile so cheerful.
I am so lucky to call her mine.
Words alone can't describe
Her talents, her beauty, or her love.

Cheriyan Kalayil Alex
8 C

THE LIGHT OF MY LIFE

My Mom is like a river that flows,
And the amount of things that she shows,
For us to become better people,
And to even help the cripple.

My Mother is a candle with fragrance,
Spreading light and fragrance to everyone,
She teaches us the same,
To not bring us any shame.

She's the rainbow of the family,
Because she keeps us all happy,
Without her sadness would spread,
And she would keep our mood far from dead.

If we are the tree she is the roots,
Because she keeps us alive,
She makes us bear some nicest fruits,
And if sadness is there the happiness will be revived.

Rifna Fathima
8 M

MOTHER'S LOVE

In the garden of love, where blossoms bloom,
A mother's heart, a comforting room.
With a gentle touch and heartfelt care,
She shares her love in every prayer.
Through stormy nights and sunny days,
Her guiding light in countless ways.
In her hug, our worries ease,
Her love, a bond that will never cease.
With soft whispers and a gentle touch,
She guides us to dream and embrace.
The stars above, our dreams so high,
With her by our side, we'll touch the sky.
Oh, dear mother, our guiding light,
Your love, a beacon shining bright.
In every moment, in every sight,
Your love forever will always shine.
You always stop and listen,
To my triumphs and fears,

Encouraging and teaching me,
And sometimes drying my tears.
And if sometimes I forget to tell you,
I truly hope you see,
I appreciate all the things you do,
And you mean the world to me.
I know I can't express it all in words,
But still, I LOVE YOU!!!

Vaishnav. R
8 C

MOTHER:
THE ICON OF LOVE

Showering you with care,
Caressing through the hair.
She's been there for you every time,
Taught you every rhyme.
To make you feel the best,
Not a single day did she rest.
She toils day and night,
To make your future bright.
Superheroes who've got warm hearts,
And sing lullabies like birds.
Teaches you the way of life,
And makes you feel so safe.
MOTHER, the icon of love,
Who came to my life like a dove...

Emin Rose
8 N

A MOTHER'S LOVE
UNSPOKEN

In this world of day and night,
You are the light that shines in my heart.
You bring grace and love
When I am mournful and dim.

Your soprano voice has helped me laugh
And your hugs have consoled me.
Your hands work and never tire;
You help me in my biggest storms.

You work through endless sleepless nights,
With your hands working like machines.
You taught me how to stand up tall,
And you nurture me with care.

You guide me with your love and devotion;
Your heart is pure and true.
Oh' mother, you are a gift beyond comparison.
You're the treasure I hold dear.

Alfie Steena
7 R

MOTHER'S HEART

In the quiet of dawn's embrace,
A mother stirs, her love ablaze.
Her hands, weathered yet tender,
Weave dreams and mend splendor.
She cooks magic in the kitchen's heat,
Turning simple ingredients into a feast.
Her laughter, a sunbeam's sweet retreat,
Guides us through life's endless lease.
Her eyes hold stories etched with care,
A lighthouse in storms, unwavering and rare.
Her love, a melody we'll forever share,
For a mother's heart knows no despair.

Muhammed Armaan
7 A

MY FEELINGS FOR MY MOM

My mother's love is pure and deep,
A love that can't be broken.
A story full of joy and care,
A bond that means the world to me.

When I'm scared or feeling sad,
She's always there to comfort me.
Her words are soft and kind,
And I wonder how I'll ever pay her back.

Sometimes I think about how moms
Ask for nothing in return,
Except for love when they need us most.

She's like a hero who plays many roles—
A doctor when we're sick,
A teacher for exams and school tests,
And a friend I can talk to anytime.

Yes, sometimes she can be annoying,
But it's only because she wants the best for us.

Happy Mother's Day to all the heroes—
Or should I say, superhero moms.

 'Cradle of Love: A Tribute to Metropolitan Moms'

Ayshath Sana Sideek
7 R

LIFE OF MOTHER

Love of Mother
She has been my best friend,
Even though she scolds me, she always loves me.
Love of Mother
She has made sacrifices for me;
If I am not feeling well,
Her eyes will turn tearful.
Love of Mother
She shines like a diamond.
If she is emotional,
She hides it from us.
Love of Mother is divine!

Abdullah Farhan
7 A

A MOTHER'S TRUE LOVE

A mother's true love,
A gift that no words
Can ever explain.

Where does she find
The strength and grace
To be our teacher, nurse, and friend?

Her voice, so kind,
So soft and warm,
It makes me wonder—
How could I ever repay her?

When I ask,
"Mom, what can I do for you?"
She smiles and says,
"I only need your true love,
That's all I want from you."

Yes, sometimes she may get mad,
But only because she wants me to be
The best person I can ever be.

Isabella sunil Mathew
7 P

A MOTHER'S LOVE

With gentle hands and a loving gaze,
A mother's care lights up our days.
Her strength, her wisdom, her tender touch,
A guiding star we love so much.
Through laughter's chime and tearful rain,
A mother's love will forever remain.
A patient heart, a calming voice,
A mother's love is our happy choice.
Happy Mother's Day to all the amazing mothers in the
world.

Niya Jyothish
7 P

I LOVE MY MOM

Mother's Day is a precious day in the world.
It is celebrated on the second Sunday
Of May.
A mother is a precious gift from
God.
Mother's Day is the perfect day
To remind us.
Mother's Day honors the hard work, love, and care
Of all mothers.
God gives us mothers like
Angels.
Having a mother like you is a blessing.
A mother is a hero in our
Life.
I love my mom.

Haya Mohammed
7 R

MOM, I LOVE YOU
TO THE MOON

I love you to the moon and back.
It's a phrase that seems hack,
But it's true, Mom, with all my heart—
You're the one who's been there from the start.
You held my hand when I was small,
And taught me how to stand tall.
You gave me wings to fly so high,
And caught me when I fell from the sky.
You've been my rock, my guiding light,
Through every day and every night.
You've cheered me on and wiped my tears,
And chased away all my fears.
Your love for me is endless and pure,
A bond that nothing can obscure.
It reaches to the moon and beyond,
And as this is your special day, I say:
Happy Mother's Day, Mom.

Jiwel
7 N

THANK YOU!

Oh mother! Oh mother!
The dignity of faith,
A force so strong,
Something I can never relate.
That joyful smile,
That sparkling soul,
Your words of style,
That make me sold.
That blind love
You gave me,
That values more than diamonds
And everything around me.
I thank you for your love,
That you gave to no one
But to me, oh mother!
I love you so much!

Ayaan Saju
7 F

MARVELOUS MOTHERS!

Starting with the poem, I have to say
Our mother she loves us everyday
Tis' true she scold us for us
Because she's hoping the best for us.

Starting with the laundry, then to cleaning
The clothes that she do, is never ending.

Qualities of our mother, will never stop
Because all new things continuously pop!
Life without a mother is always sorrow,
Because there is no mother, which we can just borrow.

Hina Farooke
7 N

MOM'S LOVE:
OUR GUIDING LIGHT

In Mom's hug, love feels brand new,
Her smile brightens skies of blue.
With her, each day is a sunny scene,
In her love, we find all we need.
Her eyes hold dreams, big and bright,
Guiding us through day and night.
With her, we soar, like birds on high,
In her embrace, we touch the sky.
For all she gives, for all she's worth,
In Mom's love, we find our mirth.
Simple joys, in her love, we see,
For in Mom's arms, we're truly free.

Parvathi Vinesh Menon
7 R

MY GUIDING LIGHT

My mother shines as my beacon of light.
She shapes my future and makes it look bright,
She taught me to be kind,
My mother is behind all my victories.

My mother taught me Maths,
And many more interesting facts.
My mother taught me to walk,
And then helped me to talk.

Her words are like honey ,
She works very hard to make money.
She is my role model,
She's the beacon: guiding my soul.

She turns my wrongs into rights.
She is always calm and never fights.
Through every plight, she shines so bright,
My mother is my guiding light.

Aysha.M
7 M

MY MOTHER

My mother, she teaches me things
That I never knew.
It is her first time
Being a mother,
And still she tries her best.
She lives for her kids
More than for herself.
Even if her life is a trial,
She makes mine the finest.
Sometimes she scolds me,
Not because she is
Displeased with me,
But because she is concerned
About me.
She chooses the best for me.
My success is also her achievement.
Nothing is greater than
The love of a real mother.

Nadha Fathima
7 P

MOMMY

No matter how many times we argue,
how many times I don't understand you,
and how many times I get scolded by you.
But I know you are always by my side,
to give me support, confidence, and care.
You always provide stability for our family,
full of laughter, full of tears, full of love.
You always stop and listen
to my triumphs and fears,
encouraging and teaching me,
and sometimes drying my tears.
And if sometimes I forget to tell you,
I truly hope you see,
I appreciate all the things you do,
and you mean the world to me.
I know I can't express everything in these words,
but still, I LOVE YOU!!

Rahila Syed
7 R

MOTHER

Your love is like moonlight,
turning harsh things into something beautiful.
A mother's love is like an island in life's ocean.
The world is a brighter place because of your love, Mom.
Your smile makes the surroundings pleasant,
your laughter can remove sadness,
and your hugs can make everything perfect.
For me, every day feels like Mother's Day.
There is no specific day needed to express my love for
you.
My heart is filled with joy and happiness
to have such a wonderful, caring, amazing, and loving
mother.
We can't imagine life without you.

S.Shithika
7 M

FATHER AND MOTHER:
MY WORLD OF JOY

Father and Mother are my family, my world of joy.
Sacrifice is a word that completely defines our mother,
And struggle is a word that perfectly describes our father.
Mom, whose name is Sneha, embodies love in its purest
form,
The first angel I saw at my very first sight in this world,
The most beautiful sight ever.
Her voice was the first I heard while I was in her womb;
She explained everything to me, even before I was born.
She cared for me deeply when I was growing inside her,
More than her own health.
Though she carried me for only seven months,
When most moms carry for nine,
I came into this world at 30 weeks, weighing 1.5 kg,
Like a tiny carrot.
She witnessed my growth for two months outside her
womb;

Her arms and chest gave me warmth, just like her womb.
As a single mother, she struggled greatly for me.
When I write these lines, I cannot move on without
mentioning my dad,
The one who came like a god into our lives to hold us
lifelong.
Mom will be complete only with our superhero, Daddy.
Mom, with her love, care, shouts, and too much fun,
Is my most super bold lady hero.
Her smile, sound, smell, and touch have been the same
From the first day I recognized her outside the womb until
today.
The most lovable and peaceful moment is when she hugs
me
After scolding me for my wrongs.
I know she shouts at me because she loves me more than
anything in this world,
Holding me tightly in every bad situation she faces.
I want to be like her

Sara Mohammed
6 N

HAPPY MOTHER'S DAY

Mom's love always shines bright,
In the morning light.
Her hugs feel very warm and tight,
It makes everything feel right.
On this special day, all of us say,
Thanks in every way,
For all you do, come what may.
Happy Mother's Day, In every single way,
You're loved more than words can say,
Forever and always, come what may.

Aditi Vipin
6 M

MY MOTHER

I LOVE YOU, MOM, FOREVER
My mom's hugs make me happy.
When I need help,
my mom is always there for me.
She is a teacher who helps me with my studies.
She is a friend with whom I can share everything.
She is a nurse who takes care of me when I am not well.
She is a chef who cooks food for me.
She is a mentor.
I am blessed to have a mom like her.
My mom makes me happy
when I am sad.
I thank her for everything
she has done for me.
She is the best mom in the world.
Happy Mother's Day!
Love you so much, Mom.

Ameen Zayed
6 D

MY MOTHER

I woke to life because of her, my mother,
She brought me forth into this world of light,
With gentle hands, she clothed me, fed me well,
Her love, a constant guide upon my path.
She kindled dreams within my eager heart,
And strove with all her strength to see them bloom.
Her spirit shines, the beacon of my soul,
The best of all, my anchor in the storm.
She carried me for ten long months, and more,
Through trials borne with grace, she labored hard.
She taught me first to form the words I speak,
To seek the joys that fill her heart with pride.
I strive to bring her happiness each day,
For all she's given, all she's sacrificed.
In gratitude, I pledge to honor her,
And make my dreams a mirror of her love.

Amila kaheesha
6 R

MY GUIDING LIGHT

The one who wants to see me smile,
The one who lights up my darkness,
The one who listens to me even in her
busyness,
The one who is my best teacher,
The one who is my only backbone,
The one who guides me to success,
The one who is there when I need her,
The one who cheers me up in my sorrow,
The one who is my shining star,
The one with the most beautiful heart,
The one who is patient—
That is none other than my mother.

Amna Ahmed
6 N

MOTHER

A mother is like a flower,
Who blooms with care.
A mother is like the sun,
Who fills hearts with light.
A mother is like a star,
Who twinkles bright at night.
A mother is like a humble leaf,
Who moves along the wind.
A mother is like the sea,
Who sings for her children,
Like the gushing sound of the waves.

Ayshath Nasha
6 Q

MOTHER'S LOVE

In her smile, a world unfolds,
Love unspoken, stories untold.
With gentle hands and eyes so kind,
In her embrace, solace I find.

Through laughter and tears, always there,
Guiding with love, tender and rare.
In each moment, her wisdom bright,
A beacon of hope in the darkest night.

Her love, a melody, sweet and true,
In every note, a bond renewed.
Grateful for her love, endlessly.

Dhiya Fathima
6 M

LOVE YOU MOTHER

Oh mother,
Oh mother,
I love you so much.
Your love is so sweet
and pure; it's like honey
on a honeycomb.
I am like a flower
nurtured with
love by you.
You're the sunshine
that lights my day.
Your love never ends.
I love you, my dear
mother ♥ ♥

Filza Fathima
6 R

MY MOTHER

My mom is great;
She's as sweet as she can be.
When I need help,
I know she is always there for me.
Mom loves her time,
even when I disturb her.
She always takes good care of me.
My mother is the best.
Mother is the name for God
in the lips and hearts of little children.
I love you, I love you, Mom.
You are the best.
You are my life.
You are my everything,
as everyone tells me. I love you.

Muhamed Hamdan
6 E

♥ M•O•M ♥

"**M**other" sounds like a small word,
But to me it means the whole world.

Don't think I hate you.
I appreciate the fact that your love is in queue.
Things that you do for me,
Is same like the honey with bee.
Mom, you loved me first,
Now and forever.

Your love is so pure and new,
Mothers hugging, kissing and loving isn't few.
And scolding of mom is the best part,
Which we can't depart.
Let us honour your love.
Let this love, never fall down or tear apart.

Niba Nourin
6 N

HAPPY MOTHER'S DAY♥

My mother is my soul,
My mother is my world,
My mother is my life,
My mother is my all.
Without my mother, I'm nothing. ♥

Adam Zayn Arshid
6 A

MOTHER MELODY

With every grin, with every tear,
Your love for me is always near.
When darkness looms, you lift me high,

In your hug, worries bid goodbye.
Your gentle touch, like a guiding star,
Through life journey, you're never far.
In stormy times or skies so clear,
Your presence soothes and quells any fear.

Your laughter, a melody, sweet and bright,
Your strength, my fortress, shining light.
For all you do, for all you are,
My love for you is like a guiding star.
On **Mother's Day**, with all my might,
I thank you, Mom, for your endless light.

Muskan.V.N
6 N

MOTHER'S LOVE :
A SONNET OF GRATITUDE

In May, we honor mothers dear,
With hearts full of love, sincere.
Their warmth, their care, their gentle ways,
Deserve our praise in endless arrays.
They kiss our wounds, they dry our tears,
Guiding us through both joys and fears.
Their laughter fills our home with light,
Their wisdom guides us through the night.
On Mother's Day, let's show our gratitude,
With flowers, hugs, and heartfelt attitude.
For all the sacrifices they have made,
In every role, they've gracefully played.
Mothers are strong and kind,
In every memory, they're enshrined.
Today and always, let's celebrate,
The love of mothers, truly great.

Aysha Fahima
6 R

MY LOVING MOTHER

My mother, my friend,

So dear, through my life, you're always near.
A tender smile to guide my way,
You're the sunshine to light my day.

A mother who always cares,
A mother who's always there.
A mother who always prays,
A mother who always stays.

When things get tough,
When all is just too much to fear,
God's words she shares,
God's light she shines.
So blessed, God made this mother mine.

A tender smile to guide my way,
You're the sunshine to light my day.
Your love has never fallen short,
You have been my only support.

Kanika M Shetty
6 N

MY MOTHER

My mom is the best,
She always gives me tests.
And when I get good marks,
She takes me to the park.
She is always busy,
Making our work easy.
Her work is very hard,
But she'll always be our security guard.

She sends us to school,
Teaching us all the rules.
I love you, Mom,
And let our bond stay strong.
Mom, you keep working day and night,
These words describe you right.
Mom, you're so hard-working,
And I love you from the bottom of my heart.

Chinmaya Joji
6 Q

MY MOTHER

Red, blue, pink, and white,
she is beautiful and loving.
She works all day and night
To make my future bright.
When I close my eyes,
She stays with me all the time.
She is in my heart and,
shines like sunshine.
She always makes me smile
and is my best friend.
She loves me from her heart,
and I see her in the night sky,
like the shining stars.
She makes my day and
prays for me every day.

Jaiveer
6 D

MY MOTHER

I woke up in the world because of my mother.
My mother brought me to this beautiful world.
My mother fed me, brought me new cloths.
My mother taught me to dream,
My mother tried her best to make my dreams true.
My mother is the best always.

My mother brought me to this world
Struggled a complete ten years to do so
My mother taught me the first word
What I do to make my mother happy
What make my mother feel proud
Afterall I am the one she gave her everything
I will try my best to make you happy mom.

Saira Mariam Ullas
6 P

MY MOTHER

You hug me tight
With all your might,
You guide me through the night sky,
Cuddling close, don't lose your hold,
For all that's left is you.
Dear Mother, your tears flow like water,
You bring joy and laughter,
Making me grow as tall as a tree.
I proudly say you are my
Guiding Star.

Zoya Adnan
6 N

MOTHER
- A HEAVEN ON EARTH

Her love is the greatest of them all.
Her hugs are warm and true,
Her voice smooth like velvet, too.
Through laughter and tears, she stands strong,
A protector and friend all day long.
Guiding us through each dream,
In her eyes, pure love brightly gleams.
We find peace in her embrace,
Her love for us will never cease.
Through thick and thin, she's always there,
With every heartbeat, she's our guide and care.
A mother's love is like no other,
Strong and kind, like no other.
They are the pillars of our hearts and minds,
Their love like stars that brightly shine.
Mother is a blessing that no one can replace.

Divaritika Sureshkumar
5 R

A MOTHERS LOVE
OUR SWEETEST GIFT

A Mother's love, aprecious gem
A Timeless gift, A diamond
Her tender heart, her gentle ways,
Illuminate our darkest days.
Her smile, a sunbeam warm bright,
Trasforms our lives, dispels the night
Her lullabies, a soothing balm
Her presence pure, A perfect calm.
With every kiss, a world of care,
In every hug, Her love laid bare.
Her voice, a melody so sweet,
In her embeace, we are complete.
To mothers dar, our endless cheer.
Our gratitude is crystal clear.
For all you give for all you do,
Our sweetest love belongs to you.

Aliya Ahmed
5 P

MOTHER

Mothers are like the oceans,
with endless love.
She teaches my heart,
like the gushing winds.
She wipes away my tears with hands,
soft like the sand.
She gleams at me,
like the twinkling stars.
Her hugs are like
the warmth of the sun.
Her voice is soothing,
like the waves.

Chris Simon Sumesh
5 E

MOM

You are my strength.
You are my wavelength.
You give me power,
And makes me bloom like a flower

You give me happiness,
Always show kindness.
You forget sufferings,
And make my life glittering.

And always being amazing mom!
Thinking my future with subtract and sum.
Encouraging me is a part of your life,
And never let me fall in trife.

Ali Hamdan
5 F

MY MOM

God has sent an angel onto the earth,
Who gave us birth.
They took care of us,
And that's our 'mom'.
A person who is valuable,
A nightingale who sings for us,
A doctor who looks for us,
A teacher who teaches us,
That's our 'mom'
Nobody can be compared to her.
She is our guardian angel.
That's our 'mother'
She tries hard to
Make our future bright
She doesn't take enough rest
She tries to do her best.
She protects us from harm.
She wishes us luck.

We should make her happy.
Because she works hard for us.
But she is our mom.
We are her children.
She wishes us well.
She is the greatest person.
I have never seen
That is my mom.

Verdil Samuel
5 H

MOM!!!

Everything changes around me..
Weather changes from hot, cold & spring....
Here is thank you song today that I will sing...

Trees from small to big... grows,
so do your love that you always show.

Days turn into night..
you are always in front of my eyes.

River becomes the ocean...
you bright up every occasion.

God can't be everywhere, so he made you...
sorry God I love my mother more than you...

Happy Mother's Day mom...may you always live long!
I love you.

Aarush
5 F

DEAR MOTHER

You are working hard for me,
and taking care of me so much.
You make good and healthy food,
even buying me everything that I say.
I love you so much.
You're my best mother,
taking me to different places like,
the park and to see my friends,
so I can enjoy. You help me study,
which is why I got great marks on tests and exams.
You sacrifice for me and make me happy,
so I love you so much.

With love

Dishan Chandra
5 E

HAPPY MOTHER'S DAY

I'm like a tree sapling;
You planted me and I
Grew because of your care;

And your love,
I shall never leave;
and forget you
Until my last breath;
You're my sunshine;

And you're the one;
Who guided the Time
when I was sad, and Lonely;
I shall never Forget you,
love you my Mom.
You're the best Mom ever.

Fathimath Nazha.P
5 R

MY MOTHER IS A BUTTERFLY

Mother, Mother,
The word is shining,
The sound seems kind,
Everyone knows her.
She is beautiful,
She is kind,
She is mother who calls us dear.
The sun rises in the morning,
But it disappears at night,
The flowers bloom like her,
The butterflies fly like her.
Angels surround her,
The sound of bird she has,
The eyes are like a mermaid's gaze.
Mother Mother,
The word is shining.

Fayha firos
5 R

MY MOM

My mom is the best.
She never rests. She works hard day and night
just to make my future very bright.
When I'm sick, she is there;
she stays up all night taking care.
I love you, Mom. You always help me
with my tests and other things.
Sometimes the marks aren't the best,
but you make me feel loved every time
you hug me or just look at me.
I love you, Mom.
Sometimes you sacrifice a lot for me.
I love you, Mom, and I cherish you
just because you are my mom.
Happy Mother's Day!
I love you, Mom.

Gaurinandhana.P. S

5 P

"BEATS OF MY HEART"

Beep, Beep, Beep
Can you hear that sound?
Yes! We can, but we can't see.
Oh! When the sound stops, we will die.
You know, the only thing in our lives like that is our
"mother."
Like our hearts are purifying blood
Our "mother" rectifies our character.
In fact, without us saying anything
She knows our movements and what we want.
If we make a mistake, she will shout at you.
But it's for our goodness.
From morning until night, she repeats the time every day.
Still, I don't know why she does that.
Oh, no, sometimes it's irritating.
But if she stops all of this,
We can't even think of that.
When the beat stops, it's like I'm dead.
Wherever I go, I want my mother, like my heart beats.

Haani Muhammed
5 J

MY LOVELY MOTHER

My mother is my first friend.
My mother is my heart.
My mother is the best;
she never ever rests.

My mother is my world;
she cares for me always.
You are my mother; I
don't need any other.

She plays with me,
She helps me with studying.
I love my mother,
I love her forever.

She is my hope, Mother.
My dear mother, you are so kind.
You are my joy.

Haniya fathima
5 R

MY MOTHER

Mom, Mom, you are the world to us.
You show us the things around us
and make us happier than others.
Whenever we are doing anything,
you support us like no one else.
Without your support, we wouldn't grow.

Krithika Rajesh
5 Q

MY MOM

My mom is so sweet,
She is a treat to the family!
She is just like how I'm saying!
Caring and sharing
The best mom I'm having!
Who teaches me, guides me,
Supports me, when I'm swaying!
She pampers me,
Cuddles me!
Kisses me and hugs me
It's her love that I'm cherishing!
My mom is adorable,
To love her is unstoppable
She belongs to me, and it feels so amazing!

Mahd Rafan
5 G

MY MOTHER

My mom is great
She'll always take care of me,
Even when I'm a pest,
My mom will take care of me the best;
Her smile is made of sunshine,
Molded with a warm heart made of pure gold,
My mom gave me a fun time;
I will love you forever,
For love is all you taught,
And love is what I earned,
I have so many things to learn;
That I yet don't understand,

Jiwon Jose
5 D

MOTHER

Why did you leave me?
The gratitude you showed me
And the love that you showered me with,
Now I remember it.
The ungrateful thing that I did to you,
Why was I like that?
Now I regret everything.
I wish you could just come back.
O Mother, if you were here,
I would feel so much love.
The greatness of your face,
O MOTHER, O MOTHER,
That reminds me of the past.
Now I just want to see you.
If you come again in a new life,
I am sure you will not remember me,
But I will remember you for centuries and centuries.
Please forgive me for the anger that I showed you.

O Mother, now I am just sad.
I can only remember the past,
Crying every day nonstop.
I just can't stop.
Now I don't even remember my siblings.
Now I just want you,
It's like a living nightmare,
Dreaming about you every day,
O Mother, O Mother.

Ishan. M
5 D

MY GOLDEN SOLACE

God has made a wonderful mother.
He molded her heart of pure gold.
I am lucky to have a mother like her.
Her arms are always open when I need a hug.
She understands whenever I need something.
I feel solace whenever my mother is with me.
Of all the special joys in life,
a mother's love and tenderness are the best of all.
She is very special to me.
And I always love my dear mother.

Dakshan.T.K
5 B

MY MOM

My mother is my world.
She is my real gold.
My mother is the best.
Not a single day she rests.
She works day and night.
To make my future very bright.
She is so kind.
She gives me strength to fight.
So that I can be the shining light.
One day when I grow up.
I will become the person that she can be proud of.
She is so honest.
She always helps me to do things.
She is so pretty.
She always gives me medicine when I am sick.
She always takes care of me.

Raizan Muhammed
5 J

MY MOTHER

My Mother is the best.
She never ever rests.
She works hard every day
To make my future very bright.
She teaches me new things every day
And there is always time to play.
She acts like a teacher to me
That's why I am not afraid to be me.
One day I will repay all her sacrifices.
I am proud that she is my mother
And I thank her every day
For her love and care forever.
I'm so grateful to have a mom like you.
You will always be my number one.
She is very beautiful and kind.
Her name is Thajeeba.

Natasha Parakkunnath
5 S

MY MOM

Oh Mom,
You love me always, right? So please forgive me tight
For all the mistakes I've made in your sight
I know you always give me special love .
I love you no matter what,
Your cuddles are really special,
And your love is like the moonlight .
You always calm me down,
Your words are really special.
Your presence makes me happy,
Your care is spectacular .
I always shine so bright,
Just because of your light .
I love you so much,
Happy mother's day!

Hrithik V
5 B

MY GUIDING STAR - MY MOM

My mother's love is like a star
Its roots are deep and strong
My mother's love is like a sea
Vast and deep, and waters flow

My mother's love is like a sun
Shining brightly from afar
My mother's love is like a rose
So tender, soft and sweet

My mother's love is like a tissue
to wipe, relax and care
My mother's love is higher than a
Mountain, and deeper than a sea.

Yuzaira Fathima
5 M

MY MOTHER

My mother, My mother.
She is pretty like no one else.
She cares me like no one else .
She gives me wings so I can flutter.
She helps me reach the clouds.
My love for her is bigger than a crowd.
Whenever I am lost.
I will find my way to you.
Even if it's a big queue.
Or just a few.
When I see you, I smile.
Even if I am far than a hundred mile.
My mother, my mother
I love you like no other.

Aaliya Sahid
4 G

MY ANGEL

Mom you're my Angel
You have always been there for me
no matter what.
You're my first friend,
my best friend
And
my forever friend.
My happiness is your happiness
My joy is your joy.
I wish I was like you
Because
Your beautiful, loving, truthful, kind
And
Best of all my mother.
No one can replace you
No one can take your place
And
No one can take me away from you.

I will always love you
no matter what
&
Happy Mother's Day...

Amreen Hajrah
4 P

LOVELY MOM

My mom is very good
I am so happy to see my mom
My mom helps me every time.
My mom is so kind, beautiful and lovely.
In her hugs, love grows tall,
My Mom is the best, above all.
Her smile shines like the sun,
With her every day is fun.
She helps me when things go wrong,
With her, we're always strong.
Mom's love, like a cosy nest,
On Mother's Day, she's the best!

Anvid Jayin
4 H

MY MOM

A mother's love,
Is like a feather
Soft and beautiful
We don't get that love
from anywhere.

Mother's love is,
Like a gem
It shines brightly.

Mother works hard for us.
Mother works day and night for us,
Without hesitation

No matter how much we thank her,
There is nothing on
Earth equal to mother's Love

Isha Mehrin
4 R

MY MOTHER

You were my first home, my shelter from the rain.
When I took my first breath,
your whole life changed,
when I cried my first tears,
you could feel my pain.
When I took my first steps,
you were up for the chase,
when I learned my first words,
We talked and we sang.
Oh, how you've loved me,
through every stage,
Oh, how you've been there, at every age.
I started school when the leaves and weather changed.
You packed me a big lunch, and wished me a great day.
You did all household chores, after working all day.
Then you hugged me and made me feel safe.
Oh, how you've loved me, through every stage,
Oh, how you've been there, at every age.
You asked me how the school was, I said, "it was okay".

I told you annoyed me, but your love remained..
I asked for some money, I started to change,
you told me I'd grow up and grow out of this phase.
I hung out with friends, set the city on fire.
I had no direction; my life was amazed.
You told me go after what made me afraid,
that dreams are worth chasing, and that I'm not my
mistakes.
You told me my hard work would pay off one day,
that struggles and hard times were never in vain.

 'Cradle of Love: A Tribute to Metropolitan Moms'

Haleema Beevi
4 A

THANK YOU, MOM

Oh, my mother, oh my mother
You brought me to this world
Oh, my mother, oh my mother
You loved me
Oh, my mother, oh my mother
You guided me to the right path
Oh, my mother, oh my mother
You taught me the right things
Oh, my mother, oh my mother
You make me so happy
Oh, my mother, oh my mother
You are my best friend
Oh, my mother, oh my mother
You are my world
Oh, my mother, oh my mother
I LOVE YOU!

Ayana Iqbal
4 E

MOM

My mom!

I want to tell you how much I love you!
I never ever told you how much I love you.
I need to let you know how much you really mean to me!
You have always been there for me when I needed you;
You are more than a friend!
Anytime I need someone to talk to,
you're always there to help me through.
Your arms were always open when I needed a hug;
Your heart understood when I needed a friend;
Your strength and love have guided me
and gave me wings to fly!
When I see all the things you do!
I can tell your love for me is true.
In this whole world there are many mothers.
I am lucky and glad to be your child
and to have such a nice mother!
I thank GOD; he gave me you!
So, this poem is dedicated to you thank you.

Fathima Naifah
4 E

I LOVE YOU MOMMY SONG

I love you mommy,
my sweet, sweet mommy.
You make me happy when I feel sad.
You took care of me when I was a baby,
So be with me forever.
You are my first friend I have ever met
and you fill our hearts with joy.
I love you mommy,
my sweet, sweet mommy.
You are my best friend since I was small.
You make me cry,
you make me laugh
and you always know how to make me feel better,
So, I want you to be free forever.
I love you mommy,
my sweet, sweet mommy.
You are my shooting star from the universe.
You came to earth to save and love us.

So, I will never forget your love that you gave me.
You are my well-wisher and you're my backbone.
I love you mommy.
Happy Mother's Day to all the wonderful mothers in the
world.

Sreeyuktha.K.S
4 J

MY SWEET MOM

My dear sweet mom, I love you so much
I don't know how much I love you.
You are so beautiful.
I really admire you in many ways,
I know that you will be there for me.
You are so caring, loveable and kind ..
I can't express in words regarding your feelings towards
me.
Because you are so good.
You can read my heart by looking into my eyes.
That much you know me, my sweet mother.
When I am sick, your warm hug is my best medicine.
You teach me good things.
You are my strength.
You are my biggest support.
You are the best mom.
Once again, I love you my sweet mom.

Nidhi Ragesh
4 H

MY MOTHER, MY STAR

My mother, My friend
You are with me till the end.
You bring me joy, you bring me hope,
Mother, you are the best.

With you I feel blessed
You are my guiding light.
In dark times you shine bright.

You catch me when I fall,
You help me stand tall.
You are a star, my superstar.
You chase my fears away.
You are the best mother, it's clear.

On this special day, I want to say,
Thank you in every way.
For all you do.

Jinaan Bint Jaseel
4 R

FOR YOU MOM..

My dear and loving mom
Thank you, a lot, for all the little work and love you give
me
Your food tastes amazing.
You help me with my homework.
You take me wherever I want to go
You are smart.
You are great.
I just want to say I love you.
You are so special and a true blessing from above
You are like a superhero.
You are the best and amazing mom I have ever met
Thank you, a lot, for caring us.
Please know that I appreciate all the things
that you do for me.
Mom, your love towards me is a special love
It inspires me each day.

Amaya Choudhary
4 M

MY MOTHER A BLESSING

Mother, what a beautiful name and beautiful person
gifted by God
She herself is the best and makes me the best.
First to wake up early in the morning
And the last to go to bed.
Busy all day with the house work,
Without her everything gets messed up.
It's only Mother's love which is so pure,
That my respect for her grows more and more.
My mother shines like a sun for me in the day,
and like a brightest star at the night.
To see happiness on my face, she smiles even in the pain.
My mother always cares and she is always there.
When things get difficult, for me she always prays.
Like God's light she shines,
I am so blessed that she is mine.

Lakshmi Reghunandanan
4-G

MY MOTHER

My Mom is great,
With none to hate.
Her arms are always open,
When I need a hug.
Mother is important in everyone's life.
She is always ready to give,whatever Ineed.
She is a source of comfort.
She is a caretaker and a teacher,
Who thought me things, in better ways.
When I need help, she will be always with me........

Ashlin Maria Anish
4 J

MY MOTHER MY GUARDIAN

My mother is really great……

She is my caretaker and my teacher
who taught me everything
When I need help she always helps me
My mother is my sunshine to light my day **
My mother is the best,
your strength and love has guided me for 10 years!!!
If I had choice of mothers you will be the one
I will select
My mother 's love is like a moon light…
You are the best…
You're amazing, it's true.
Thank you for everything…
Happy mother's day.

Saiha T Sunil
4 G

MY LOVELY MOTHER

My lovely mother.
She took care of me when i was young.
A mother's love is the purest love.
She never lies to me.
She is like a fairy from my heart.
I want to be like her when i grow up.
She is my destiny to succeed.
I love her with all my heart.
I will never let her down.
She is the best.
She is my lovely mother.
I see her like an angel in my eyes.
I love her so so much.

Shanza Mehrin
4 E

MY WONDERFUL MOTHER

God made a wonderful mother
A mother who is optimistic
He made her smile out of sunshine
And he molded her heart of pure gold
In her eyes he placed bright shining stars.
In her cheeks fair roses you see
God made a wonderful mother
And he gave that dear mother to me.
Thank you mom for everything that you do
and for your never ending love.
You are so special.
A true blessing From above
with all my heart I want to say
"I LOVE YOU MOM"
HAPPY MOTHERS DAY

Yuvraj Singh Mathru
4 M

TO MY MOM

In a world of colors, bright and new,
A poem for Mom, sincere and true.
With every word, I'll paint a scene,
Of a love that's pure and evergreen.

In her arms, I find solace and peace,
A love that never seems to cease.
Her gentle touch, a soothing balm,
Her voice, a sweet and tender psalm.

She's the sunshine on a cloudy day,
Guiding me along life's winding way.
No words can truly capture the grace,
The beauty of a mother's embrace.

But in this poem, I hope to convey,
The love and gratitude I feel today.
Original and unique, it's made for you,
To celebrate a love so pure and true.

Annbriya Angel
4 M

HEART OF A MOTHER

I love you mom
I love you mom
I make you glad everyday
I pray for you…

I love you mom
I love you mom
You are the shiny star in my heart
You are the queen of my heart

I love you mom
I love you mom
Because you care and love me a lot
I say sorry for my blunders

I love you mom
I love you mom
You are the Princess of my heart
Happy Mother's Day mom.

Affan Farhan
3 B

MY MOTHER

My mother is a beautiful creation,
In this selfish world she is the only
One who always wants to see you,
happy.
A Mother may be educated or not
But she is a best guide.
A mother is always an angel.

Manish Sudhakar
3 B

AMMA

In my cosy Bed, Snuggled tight,
With Amma's hugs, everything's alright.
Her smile, oh so sweet,
Makes my world complete.

Reading books, side by side,
With Amma, my joy knows no hide.
We laugh, we share, and we play,
In her arms. I'll always stay.

My Amma, My guiding light,
With you,everything feels right.
I love you more than you'll ever know,
My Amma, My love ,let it forever glow.

Aysha Ahmed
3 G

MOTHER

Mother is like a flower,
Blooming with love.
She is great with kindness,
My mother makes me happy,
And she is good.
She makes me feel better.
Mothers are the best.
Mothers are beautiful.
Mothers are sweet and caring.
Mothers are amazing.

Khadijah Waafiyah
3 N

MOTHER'S DAY SONG

I love you mommy, my sweet sweet mommy.
You always help me when I feel sad.
You are my best mommy ever.
You are my super hero.
And you help me with things great and small.
You make me laugh and when I feel sad you know how to
make me feel better.
And I love you mommy, my sweet sweet mommy and you
are my best mommy ever and ever…
la la lala lalala la lala lala…
Be with me forever in my life.

Samrah Mahek
3 A

MY MOTHER, MY ANGEL

My mother is my heaven
She is the one who looks like a twinkle star

She has the brightest face I have ever seen
She will wipe my tears when I am sad
She makes me happy

She is a sparkling gift from God
I love my mother

Dakshitha Rajil
3 F

MY DEAREST MOM

My Mommy, My Mommy,
Who always cheers me up.
She is the best.
Who always cares and loves me.
She is kind and teaches me a lot.
She is very special forever and ever.
My super woman in the world.
She cooks me what I need.
In this world, its my mom
who understands me the most.
She is a good teacher, listener,
And my ever best friend.
I love you my dear Mom.
Thank you so much for everything.
You are the best.

Aarush K.R
3 F

MY LOVELY MOTHER

My mother is my hero
She is my world.
She teaches me good things.
She helps me study even though,
She has work to do.
For the world she is just a mom,
But for our family you are our world.
I love you MOM.

Hanan Najim
3 D

MY MOM

Roses are beautiful.
Grasses are green.
Chocolates are tasty.
And you are my sweet mom.
I love you, mommy.
She loves me too much.
She cares for me too much.
I love you, mommy.

Fathima Ayra
3 D

MY MOTHER IS THE BEST

My mother is the best,
She never seems to rest.
She works hard every single day,
To make my future bright in every way.

She teaches me new things every day,
And there's always time to laugh and play.
She acts like a teacher too,
That's why I'm not afraid to be true.

One day, I'll repay her sacrifice,
For all she's done, and her advice.
I'm proud she's my mother, it's clear,
And I thank her every day, year after year.

Vashisht.C.S
3 E

MY MOTHER

My mother name is Shwetha

she is my first teacher,
With a kind and gentle touch.

she works hard everyday,
And cooks food that tastes good.
my mother is my life
I respect her very much.

Muhammed Haziq
3 M

MY MOTHER

My mother loves me a lot,
She takes care of me when I'm hurt, on the spot.
She makes delicious meals for us every day,
And helps me in every single way.

My mother is a superwoman, it's true,
She helps me with all the things I need to do.
She plays with me when I'm feeling bored,
Her love is something that can't be ignored.

She's the most beautiful one I know,
Always there to help me grow.
She tucks me in at night so tight,
And wakes me up with morning light.

She cleans the messes that I make,
And helps me learn for knowledge's sake.
She teaches me new things every day,
And guides me in a loving way.

My mother is my life, my guide, my friend,
She's the best person from start to end.
My mother is the best, the very best,
I love my mother, more than all the rest.

Mohammed Aahil Ghulam
3 N

MY MOM, THE BEST

My mom,My mom
I love you so much.
You are the best
I know you also love me too...
My mom is my first teacher ,
You take care of me at any time .
That's why I love you mom.
My mom, My mom
You are the best ..
My mom is so precious
She is the best gift in my entire life...
My mom is so special for me.
My mom,My mom
You are the best
I love you....I love you...
You teach me all the good things
You always play with me, that's why I feel so happy.
My mom, My mom
You are the best,
I love you very much.

Fatimah zahra
Grade 3D

MY LOVELY MOM

Oh, mother, your heart is pure gold.
In any way, you will be here for me.
You are calm and happy.
Your words make me warm when I'm cold.
You are sweeter than honey.
You wrap me full of joy.
I suppose you're sweet .
When I see or smell a flower.
It reminded me of you.

Danvin Nikhil
3 E

MY MOTHER

Oh mom, I Love you so much!!!
When I dive deep in the sea,
Her tears flows for me.

When I do something wrong,
She is there to teach me.

When I am sad, my mom supports me.
Oh mom, you love me so much.
Oh mom, you love me so much.

Zunaira Mehwish
Grade 3B

MY BELOVED MOTHER

"**O**o mother my beloved mother"
other names for love, caring, and support includes merely
mother.
"U are my first teacher 'Who taught me to take my first
steps,
speak my first words, and teach me about the world, both
good and bad?
"Oo mother my first doctor"
You know my ailment first, and you treat my wounds with
kisses and hugs.
My all-pain soothes and heals in your lap.
"Ooo mother my first love"
I found the purest love in your eyes.
That unconditional love makes me love you from
beginning to end.
"Ooo mother my beloved mother"
The alternative name for love, caring, and support is
"mother."

"U are my first teacherWho trains me to take my first
steps, speak my first words, and teach me about the world,
good and bad?
"Oo mother my first doctor"
You know my ailment first and heal my wound with kisses
and hugs.
In your lap, my entire pain subsides and heals.
"Oo mother my first love"
I found the purest love on earth, just in your eyes.
Your unconditional love makes me love you from the
start.
"Oo mother my first friend"
My mom is my foremost and best friend, who deeply
understands me and encourages me through difficult .